PROFESSOR PEABODY

Illustrations by [illegible] Mitson *Written by Giles Reed*

PUBLISHED BY STUDIO PUBLICATIONS (IPSWICH) LIMITED
32 PRINCES STREET, IPSWICH, SUFFOLK, ENGLAND

Peabody is one of the Munch Bunch.

He lives in an old, blue treasure chest next door to Adam Avocado.

Peabody is very clever and knows the answers to lots of questions.

His friends call him Professor Peabody.

Every morning, before he gets out of bed, Peabody reads a book.

Peabody reads lots of books.

That's why he is so clever.

Peabody also collects stamps.

And each morning, after he has read his letters, he sticks the stamps into an album.

That's how Peabody knows about every country in the world!

One morning Peabody climbed a tree to learn about birds' eggs.

He was very busy studying a nest, when he heard a loud cry.

"It sounds as if somebody is in danger," he thought.

It was Wally Walnut, Olly Onion and Casper Carrot.

They had gone for a ride down the river in an old tub.

"Please help us Professor Peabody," called Casper. "We can't stop and we're very frightened."

Peabody threw them a rope, and pulled them on to the grass.

"That was very silly of you to go on the river in that old tub," Peabody told them. "You could have been drowned."

Peabody had a book all about boats.

So they decided to make a boat for all the Munch Bunch.

Peabody worked all night drawing the plans for the new boat.

The next morning they began to make their new boat.

Peabody was busy reading his plans.

Casper, Wally and Olly were busy doing just what Peabody told them to do.

Spud and Sally Strawberry came to help.

Spud is very strong, and he put the mast into the boat all by himself.

Peabody was still busy reading his plans, making sure that everything was being done properly.

Soon it was nearly finished.

Spud and Wally were just adding the finishing touches . . .

Sally and the Banana Bunch were busy painting . . .

And Peabody was checking that Lizzie Leek was making the sail properly.

At last their shining new boat was finished.

Professor Peabody and his Munch Bunch friends were very excited.

Even Olly Onion was happy!

They fixed some wheels to the boat and pulled it down to the river.

SPLASH!

Peabody and the Banana Bunch pushed the boat into the river.

"Hooray!" the Munch Bunch cheered.

"All aboard!" shouted Peabody.

And one by one the Munch Bunch stepped onto their new boat.

They were very excited now.

At last, they sailed their new boat.

Peabody took command.

"I'm so pleased that you are clever, Professor Peabody," said Olly Onion, "because if you weren't, we would still be using that dangerous old tub for sailing on the river."

A.M.

"Well," said Peabody, "if you read more books you could be clever, too – just like me."

Acknowledgement: This story of Professor Peabody was adapted by Giles Reed, from an original idea by Elizabeth Henderson.